300 Incredible Things for Seniors on the Internet

300INCREDIBLE.COM, LLC
600 Village Trace, Building 23
Marietta, Georgia 30067

(800) 909-6505

ISBN 1-930435-04-5

— Dedication —

To our parents.

Introduction

Seniors and the Internet are a great combination. Both have much information and knowledge to share. By using this book, seniors can easily harness the power of the Internet for communication, health research, financial planning, travel arrangements and almost everything else. So, log on and experience the joy of exploration and discovery on the Net.

Joe West
JoeWest@Hereontheweb.com

Ken Leebow
Leebow@300incredible.com
http://www.300incredible.com

About the Authors

Joe West is creator and producer of HereontheWeb.com, a Web site and nationally-syndicated radio show that discover interesting, informative and fun destinations on the Internet. He began exploring the Net in the early 1990s and, like many, was amazed at the enormous amount of material available on the information superhighway. Joe has introduced thousands of people to the Net and its hidden treasures though his show and site and has written Internet-related articles for various publications. He currently resides in Los Angeles.

Ken Leebow has been involved with the computer business for over twenty years. The Internet has fascinated him since he began exploring it several years ago, and he has helped over a million readers utilize its resources. Ken has appeared frequently in the media, educating individuals about the Web's greatest hits. He is considered a leading expert on what is incredible about the Internet.

When not online, you can find Ken playing tennis, running, reading or spending time with his family. He is living proof that being addicted to the Net doesn't mean giving up on the other pleasures of life.

Acknowledgments

Putting a book together requires many expressions of appreciation. The following people deserve special thanks:

- Karen Reyes, whose expertise in gerontology helped immensely with the writing of this book.

- Margery Burt, whose helpful suggestions added greatly to the scope of this book.

- Ken's family (Denice, Alissa and Josh) for being especially supportive during the writing of the book.

- Paul Joffe and Janet Bolton, of *TBI Creative Services*, for their editing and graphics skills.

- Mark Krasner and Janice Caselli for sharing the vision of the book and helping make it a reality.

The Incredible Internet Book Series

300 Incredible Things to Do on the Internet

300 More Incredible Things to Do on the Internet

300 Incredible Things for Kids on the Internet

300 Incredible Things for Sports Fans on the Internet

300 Incredible Things for Golfers on the Internet

300 Incredible Things for Travelers on the Internet

300 Incredible Things for Health, Fitness & Diet on the Internet

300 Incredible Things for Auto Racing Fans on the Internet

300 Incredible Things for Self-Help & Wellness on the Internet

300 Incredible Things to Learn on the Internet

300 Incredible Things for Home Improvement on the Internet

300 Incredible Things for Seniors on the Internet

300 Incredible Things for Pet Lovers on the Internet

300 Incredible Things for Women on the Internet

America Online Web Site Directory
Where to Go for What You Need

TABLE OF CONTENTS

		Page	Sites

TABLE OF CONTENTS (continued)

CHAPTER I
UP & RUNNING

1
Free Internet Access

http://www.freedomlist.com
http://www.hereontheweb.com/freeinternet.htm
It almost sounds too good to be true. These sites list and rate many of the free
Internet service providers.

2
Internet 101

http://specials.about.com/channels/internet/net101
http://www.webteacher.org
http://www.newbie-u.com
http://howto.yahoo.com
Whether you're looking for a free six-week course in computers or just a few tips on
surfing the Web, you'll find what you need here.

3
Livin' Easy

http://www.livineasy.com
This site is dedicated to seniors who wish that computers and the Internet were easier to use.

4
Empowering You

http://www.seniortips.com
Find information and products that make technology more accessible and easier on the eyes, ears, hands and wallet.

5
Learn the Net

http://www.learnthenet.com
Learn the basics of e-mail, Web surfing, downloading files and more. There are also tips and tricks for experienced users.

6
By the Book

http://www.northernwebs.com/bc
This award-winning Internet tutorial is one of the oldest and most reliable on the Web. Visit Beginners Central and learn at the pace that's perfect for you.

7
Shedding Some Light

http://www.agelight.org/resources.htm
Age Light contains numerous tips and resources to help you with your computing experience. You'll also find a national directory of senior training centers that provide in-depth computer training.

8
Help on the Web

http://www.webhelp.com
http://www.askme.com
Everybody has questions now and then. These sites are staffed with real people waiting to answer yours.

9
E-Mail Assistance

http://www.emailaddresses.com
http://www.iwillfollow.com/email.htm
E-mail is the most frequently used (and abused) service on the Net. Learn just about everything you need to know here.

10
Get Plugged In

http://www.realaudio.com
http://www.shockwave.com
http://www.acrobat.com
Many Web sites offer features and functions that use the above software to play music, show flashy Web pages and open documents. If you want those capabilities, make sure you download the applications.

11
WebTV

http://www.webtv.com
With WebTV, you can access the Internet and enjoy the wonders of e-mail without having a computer.

12
Ask and You Will Receive

http://www.askjeeves.com
During your Web surfing, you will inevitably use search engines to look for specific information. Asking Jeeves will simplify the process and usually yield a better result.

13
Neat Net Tricks

http://www.neatnettricks.com
Jack Teems digs deep to expose and explain an assortment of helpful — and often hidden — features of the Internet and your computer. Sign up to receive a free, twice-monthly newsletter.

14
Download City

http://www.download.com
http://www.tucows.com
http://www.webshots.com
Downloading small programs like screen savers and desktop themes is easy, useful and fun. These sites offer hundreds of free programs for you to try.

15
<u>World Domains</u>

http://www.theodora.com/country_digraphs.html

We all know about ".com" and ".org," but did you know that every country in the world has its own unique domain suffix? Visit this site to connect all the dots to their respective countries.

CHAPTER II
SILVER SURFING

16
AARP Webplace

http://www.aarp.org

With more than 30-million members, AARP is the nation's largest organization for ages 50 and up. Learn about computers, the Internet, legislative issues important to seniors, legal help, travel and leisure activities, personal finance and more.

17
CARP

http://www.fifty-plus.net

Learn about Canada's Association for the over-fifty crowd. Enjoy chat rooms, forums and a wealth of articles about everything from money to family, or even a travel destination where you can get away from it all.

18
Seniors.com

http://www.seniors.com

This resource provides a host of interactive senior activities, such as chat, message boards and surveys. You can also research major topics from heath to travel.

19
Make a Friend

http://www.friendly4seniors.com

Meet Lori. She has categorized many sites that are senior friendly.

20
Third Age

http://www.thirdage.com

The focus here is information and introducing seniors to a way of meeting, sharing and connecting with one another. Visit this site to find fun and interesting topics.

21
Live to 100

http://www.beeson.org/Livingto100

Answer these questions to help determine how you might reach triple digits.

22
Elder Abuse Law

http://www.elderabuselaw.com

http://www.gwjapan.com/NCEA

Lean about the laws that protect seniors from physical, emotional and financial abuse. Sign up to receive a free quarterly newsletter and regular Elder Abuse Alerts.

23
Elder Law

http://www.seniorlaw.com
http://www.naela.com
These comprehensive, well-designed sites include wills, estate planning, trusts, Medicare, Medicaid, a senior law search engine and other resources.

24
Access America for Seniors

http://www.seniors.gov
You'll find timely articles of interest through this impressive online resource.

25
Seniors Search

http://www.seniorslounge.com
http://www.eldersearch.com
These search engines are designed especially for seniors and contain many other helpful features.

26
Grandparents Online

http://www.igrandparents.com
http://www.egrandparents.com
http://www.grandsplace.com
http://www.aarp.org/confacts/programs/gic.html
Get insightful news, health tips, shopping information and more, all designed with grandparents in mind.

27
50+

http://www.50on.com
http://www.go60.com
Browse through a multitude of well-researched, newsworthy and interesting topics for older adults here, including no-nonsense, straightforward resources aimed at helping seniors age with grace and success.

28
Elder Web

http://www.elderweb.com
This site states that "Most older Americans say senior years are the best time of life." Let ElderWeb fill you in on the details.

29
Senior Net

http://www.seniornet.org

This extraordinary collection of resources is aimed at enhancing the lives of older adults through the use of computer technology and the Internet. Some of the best sections include a scam and fraud center, a national learning center directory and a section dedicated to healthy aging.

30
Sites for Seniors

http://www.seniorsite.com
http://www.seniorswitch.com
http://www.seniors-site.com
http://www.seniorworld.com

Visit these sites for well-organized content, including chat rooms, message boards, entertainment guides, Ask the Experts, Senior Scam Alerts and more.

31
Grandma Knows Best

http://www.grandmabetty.com

Betty was a frustrated Internet user. Now she has a Web site that helps other seniors surf the Web successfully.

32
The Senior's Job Bank

http://www.seniorjobbank.com
Ability is ageless. This bank has a database where you can search for jobs or post your résumé.

33
Administration on Aging

http://www.aoa.gov
The AOA provides a comprehensive collection of informative articles and many links associated with aging. This site has something for everyone — aging news and statistics, anti-fraud initiatives, financial planning and more.

34
American Society on Aging

http://www.asaging.org
This site includes a wide range of informational resources related to elderly issues and is useful for caregivers and family members.

35
Yahoo for Seniors!

http://seniors.yahoo.com
The Net's premier search directory has a special section created for seniors.

36
Grand Times

http://www.grandtimes.com
Serving savvy seniors since 1995, this weekly Internet magazine is sometimes controversial, but always informative with issues, politics, leisure and more.

37
SeniorCitizens.com

http://www.seniorcitizens.com
This site's stated mission is "to provide senior citizens anywhere in the world with the information they need to enjoy the most interesting and healthy lives possible."

38
Wired Seniors

http://www.wiredseniors.com
Wired Seniors is a gateway to several other senior-related sites, including radio, search, home exchange and age of reason.

"He didn't fall in love with someone on the computer. He fell in love with the computer!"

39
All About Seniors

http://seniorliving.about.com
http://seniorhealth.about.com
http://4seniors.4anything.com
From active living to taxes, these sites will keep you in great shape.

40
Generation A

http://www.generationa.com
Here's a place you can find timely news of interest to "Gen A'ers," including health, travel, sports, entertainment and even guides to help you travel the Net.

41
Magazines Galore

http://www.newchoices.com
http://www.lhj.com/more
http://www.seasonedcitizen.com
http://www.sunset.com
These publications cover a wide range of topics for today's active senior.

42
Let's Chat About the Weather

http://www.weather.com
http://www.accuweather.com
http://www.intellicast.com
http://www.nws.noaa.gov

Everyone loves to talk about the weather. With these sites, you'll know more than your local weatherman.

43
Sports Talk

http://www.cnnsi.com
http://www.sportsline.com
http://espn.go.com

Did you miss the end of last night's game? Twenty-four hours a day, these sites report the scores and much more.

44
Enjoy the Links

http://www.golf.com
http://www.golfonline.com
http://www.golfweb.com
http://www.tigerwoods.com
When it comes to golf sites, these are the best of the Web.

45
Athletic Prowess

http://espn.go.com/sportscentury
Who were the greatest athletes of the 20th Century? ESPN has the answer.

46
I'm Retired

http://kids.infoplease.com/ipka/A0113737.html
These may not be the greatest athletes of all time, but they were good enough to have their uniform numbers retired.

CHAPTER III
THE LIFE CYCLE

47
Code of Conduct

http://www.hon.ch
http://www.hiethics.org
These organizations are taking steps to assure that health Web sites follow a code of conduct and ethics related to information and privacy. Before researching any health issue, be sure to make an appointment here.

48
Medicare

http://www.medicare.gov
This official U.S. Government site for Medicare information has everything about Medicare, Medigap and much more.

49
Surgery

http://www.yoursurgery.com
This site is designed to educate the average individual about surgery. You'll find explanations for the most commonly performed surgeries, using simple diagrams and cutting edge animation.

50
The Web MD

http://www.webmd.com
This premier health site on the Net offers information on just about every health and wellness topic available.

51
Healthwatch

http://healthwatch.medscape.com
http://www.healthatoz.com
Here are well-rounded, comprehensive health sites with A–Z health topics, daily features, ask the expert, health news and more. Another nice feature is the Health Plan Report Card that lets you compare your own health plan with others.

52
Gateway to Healthcare

http://www.healthfinder.gov
http://www.achoo.com
These sites provide a gateway to reliable consumer health and human services on the Net.

53
Intelligent Health

http://www.intelihealth.com
You'll find a special section for seniors, free health e-mails on fifteen different topics and interactive features like chat and "Ask the Doc Q & A."

54
Thrive Online

http://www.thriveonline.com
Thrive Online organizes informative heath information into seven main categories: Conditions, Medical, Fitness, Sexuality, Nutrition, Serenity and Weight.

55
Net Calls

http://www.drweil.com
http://www.drkoop.com
http://www.drruth.com
http://www.drbernie.com

Doctors may not make house calls any more, but many good ones are on the Net.

56
America's Doctor

http://www.americasdoctor.com

Can't get out to visit your doctor today? These doctors will have an online chat with you regarding your health issues.

57
The Doctor Directory

http://www.doctordirectory.com
http://www.bestdoctors.com

These easy-to-use, online directories enable you to locate the nearest specialists.

58
Online Pharmacy

http://www.rxlist.com
http://www.merck-medco.com
http://www.planetrx.com
http://www.drugstore.com

The Internet Drug Index and online pharmacies are available to you twenty-four hours a day. Learn more about medications and get your prescriptions filled online.

59
Diagnosis and Therapy

http://www.merck.com/pubs/mmanual

The world-renowned Merck Research Laboratories present "The Merck Manual of Diagnosis and Therapy," with in-depth discussions of more than 300 health topics.

60
World Health Network

http://www.worldhealth.net

The World Academy of Anti-Aging has brought together all the latest news and research related to longevity and anti-aging.

61
Health and Age

http://www.healthandage.com
The Novartis Foundation for Gerontology supports education and innovation in healthy aging, geriatrics and the care of elderly people.

62
Alzheimer's

http://www.alz.org
http://www.alzforum.org
http://www.alzheimers.com
http://www.zarcrom.com/users/yeartorem
Up-to-date, comprehensive and informative, these sites explore the latest medical and scientific news on this debilitating disease, while shedding light on the human side, with personal accounts and stories of courage.

63
Time Slips

http://www.timeslips.org
The creator of this site heads several centers where Alzheimer's sufferers are encouraged to express themselves through creativity.

64
Prostate Cancer

http://www.prostate.com
http://www.prostatecancer.on.ca
http://www.comed.com/Prostate

These are comprehensive resources dedicated to prostate health. Sections include an overview of the gland, diseases and treatment.

65
Arthritis Central

http://www.arthritiscentral.com

Get current news on this crippling disease by reading about the latest research and treatments. There's even a rheumatologist search tool.

66
Diabetes

http://www.diabetes.org
http://www.niddk.nih.gov
http://www.lillydiabetes.com

These are excellent resources for those who have Diabetes or know someone who does. Topics include nutrition, exercise, research, care and even clinical trials.

67
Heart Information

http://www.heartinfo.org

This educational site provides a wide range of information and services to heart patients and others interested in learning about lowering their risk factors for heart disease.

68
Breast Cancer

http://www.cancerhelp.com

http://www.nationalbreastcancer.org

http://www.nabco.org

Find detailed information and quick links to the very latest news in breast cancer research, prevention and treatment.

69
Nursing Home Information

http://www.nursinghomeinfo.com

http://members.tripod.com/~volfangary

Selecting a nursing home can be tedious. These sites can help make it less difficult.

70
Family Caregiver Alliance

http://www.caregiver.org
This is an excellent source for support groups, research, workshops, news and more, all aimed at long-term care.

71
Mr. Long-Term Care

http://www.mr-longtermcare.com
The following testimonial says it best: "I want to thank Mr. Long-Term Care for his commitment to improving long-term care and to educating the public about the great need for affordable quality care in this country." —Hillary Rodham Clinton.

72
Assisted Living Information

http://www.assistedlivinginfo.com
This is an online guide for selecting an assisted living facility, retirement community or other personal care facility anywhere in the United States. Several helpful tools are offered, including a map-based search engine to help find a facility near family and friends.

73
Eldercare Locator
http://www.aoa.gov/elderpage/locator.html
This site puts individuals in touch with support resources at the local level, all aimed at keeping older adults independent and comfortable in their own homes.

74
Preparing for the Inevitable
http://dying.about.com
Mortality can be a difficult subject to face, but proper planning and preparation are necessary for you and your loved ones.

75
Grieving
http://www.death-dying.com
This site provides comfort, support and education about issues surrounding death, to help people at a time when they are confused, apprehensive and dealing with shock and sorrow.

76
Federal Trade Commission
http://www.ftc.gov/bcp/rulemaking/funeral
This is a section of the official FTC Web site, which outlines the many federal laws that protect consumers in matters related to funerals.

77
Funeral Information
http://www.funerals.org
http://www.funeralnet.com
http://www.funeral.com
Visit these sites for helpful funeral planning information, tips, directories and links.

78
Internet Cremation Society
http://www.cremation.org
This site is a must for anyone considering cremation. It includes answers to some frequently asked questions and links to regional cremation societies that may help you find low cost service.

79
Ashes on the Sea
http://www.ashesonthesea.com
Ashes on the Sea offers helpful advice and information for anyone considering a "scattering" at sea.

80
National Casket Retailers Association
http://www.casketstores.com
This national directory of casket retailers offers an easy way to locate casket retailers near you.

81
Legacy
http://www.legacy.com
Legacy offers a perpetual, online memorial — a place for remembrance without the customary boundaries of space or time. You'll also find a helpful obituary finder that covers newspapers throughout the U.S. and Canada.

82
Perpetual Memorials

http://www.angelsonline.com
http://www.forevernetwork.com
http://www.cemetery.org
These sites offer virtual memorials that can include photos, audio and video.

83
Widow Net

http://www.fortnet.org/widownet
Created by and for widows and widowers, topics here include: dealing with grief, bereavement and recovery, getting through the holidays and "Public Education for the Terminally Tactless" (dumb remarks and stupid questions).

CHAPTER IV
FINANCE & INVESTMENT

84
Timely Financial News

http://www.wsj.com
http://www.barrons.com
http://www.bloomberg.com
These Wall Street watchers will keep you informed.

85
Financial Magazines

http://www.forbes.com
http://www.fortune.com
http://www.businessweek.com
http://www.worth.com
http://www.economist.com
Maintain your fortune by reading these publications online. In addition to their regular content, most offer financial tools and newsletters.

86
Minding Your Money

http://www.money.com
http://www.smartmoney.com
http://www.kiplinger.com
Personal finance magazines are online with tools, tips and everything you need.

87
On the Money

http://www.onmoney.com
Here's a one-stop solution to money management. You'll find experts, guides, news and areas to manage all aspects of your finances.

88
Terms of Investment

http://www.invest-faq.com
http://www.investopedia.com
http://www.investorwords.com
These sites will provide you with step-by-step guides, recommended reading, tips and definitions.

89
Gomez?

http://www.gomez.com
Gomez rates and ranks online banks, brokers, insurance, mortgages and much more.
There is even an Ask Gomez section where you can get answers to such questions
as, "Who is the best online broker?"

90
Knowledge Brokers

http://cbs.marketwatch.com
http://www.cnnfn.com
http://www.cnbc.com
A wealth of finance-related information is just a few clicks away. These big media
companies offer timely and detailed financial news and information.

91
Let's Talk Money

http://www.investorschat.com
http://www.raginbull.com
http://www.investingonline.org
Investment chat rooms and online investing have become unbelievably popular. Test
these sites to see if online investing is for you.

92
Research, Research, Research

http://www.justquotes.com
http://www.dailystocks.com
http://finance.yahoo.com
You can't beat these sites for researching specific stocks.

93
Invest the Like Pros

http://www.investmentdiscovery.com
This directory identifies which stocks are being purchased by specific funds.

94
Mutual Funds

http://www.findafund.com
http://www.fundalarm.com
http://www.fundsinteractive.com
The easiest way to get into the market is via mutual funds. Let these sites help you become a knowledgeable investor.

95
Investing in Bonds

http://www.bondsonline.com
http://www.investinginbonds.com
If bonds are among your investments, these sites will provide timely information.

96
What's It Worth?

http://www.ny.frb.org
Do you need to know what your savings bonds are worth? Use this quick and easy calculator from the Federal Reserve.

97
Fantasy Trading

http://game.etrade.com
http://www.fantasystockmarket.com
http://www.investorsleague.com
These sites will give you $100,000 (in virtual cash) to invest any way you want. Compete against your friends and have fun, without any risk.

98
Socially Aware

http://www.socialinvest.org

The Social Investment Forum site offers comprehensive information, contacts and resources about socially responsible investing.

99
Social Security Administration

http://www.ssa.gov

Lots of important information can be found at the official site of the Social Security Administration, including the new electronic SSA newsletter, various publications, fraud reporting, news and the latest legislation impacting the SSA.

100
Internal Revenue Service

http://www.irs.gov

Despite common fear of the IRS, this site is very helpful. Learn about electronic filing, print tax forms, learn tax tips and more.

101
Money Central Tax Help

http://moneycentral.msn.com/tax/home.asp
Money Central provides very useful tax information, including tips on how do avoid an audit, the top ten overlooked deductions and the top seven taxpayer mistakes.

102
Taxes 'R Us

http://www.taxplanet.com
http://www.taxsites.com
From current news to a year-round tax guide, you'll find several categories to keep you informed.

103
401(k)

http://www.401kafe.com
We hear about 401(k)'s all the time. Let this café provide you with tips, calculators, learning tools and timely information about these retirement accounts.

104
Retirement Sounds Great

http://www.dtonline.com/prptoc/prptoc.htm
http://4retirement.4anything.com
http://4retirementplanning.4anything.com
http://retireplan.about.com
http://financialplan.about.com
http://www.fool.com/retirement.htm

We work hard so we can enjoy retirement. Good planning helps make it all possible.

105
Save the Wealth

http://www.savewealth.com

With sections for estate planning, retirement planning, tax issues and more, this site will help you save your wealth.

106
Stretch Your Dollar

http://www.stretcher.com

The motto here is: "Living better for less." You'll find great resources for all aspects of everyday life.

107
Wills and Trusts

http://www.mtpalermo.com
This is a free crash course in wills and trusts put together by Michael Palermo, attorney and certified financial planner.

108
Estate Planning

http://www.estateplanforyou.com
http://www.estateattorney.com
http://www.freeadvice.com
http://www.nolo.com/encyclopedia/ep_ency.html
Prior, proper planning prevents problems with your estate.

109
Reverse Mortgage Resource

http://www.reverse.org
http://www.hud.gov/rmtopten.html
http://www.reverseweb.com
Everything you need to know about reverse mortgages can be found at these sites including alerts, FAQs, calculators and personal mortgage counseling.

110
HUD for Seniors

http://www.hud.gov/senior.html
HUD offers this resource to seniors for information related to housing, home loans, reverse mortgages and more. You'll also find information about senior fraud, housing discrimination and reverse mortgage scams.

111
Senior Sites

http://www.seniorsites.com
http://www.seniorresource.com
Visit these sites for valuable information related to housing options for seniors, financial planning and preparation needed to pay for housing.

112
Home on the Net

http://www.realtor.com
http://www.homeadvisor.com
There are many tools for homebuyers and sellers at these sites.

"You invested $100 a week ago and we're not rich yet. I thought you knew how to use a computer!"

113
Your Domain

http://realestate.yahoo.com
http://www.domania.com
These sites provide all the tools and information you need to save time and money in real estate. Learn about home values, schools, neighborhoods, cities and more.

CHAPTER V
BUYER BEWARE

114
Consumer World

http://www.consumerworld.org

This site boasts an impressive collection of the most useful consumer resources on the Net. You'll also find current news, a list of recent scams and helpful tips to avoid becoming a victim.

115
Consumerama

http://www.consumerama.org

Here's a consumer site with attitude! There are numerous departments, including Consumer Alert, Protest Site of the Day, Boycott Site of the Day and Attention Shoppers.

116
Consumer Reports

http://www.consumerreports.org
Whether you plan to shop online or at your favorite store down the street, this is a good place to start. Find thousands of product reviews and buying tips, all organized by category.

117
Auto Price Check

http://www.kbb.com
http://www.edmunds.com
Here are the online homes of some trustworthy publications that tell you how much vehicles are worth. Don't buy or sell a car without first checking these sites.

118
Recalls on the Net

http://www.safetyalerts.com
http://www.recalls.org
Make sure you're safe. These sites provide safety alerts and recall notices for all types of products.

119
Postal Inspectors
http://www.framed.usps.com/postalinspectors
If you're looking for information about mail fraud or want to report suspected mail fraud, this is the place to turn. You'll find answers to frequently asked questions, consumer fraud alerts and a mail fraud report form.

120
National Fraud Information Center
http://www.fraud.org
This is an excellent anti-fraud resource containing concise, easy-to-find information on fraud against the elderly, Internet fraud, telemarketing fraud and more.

121
<u>Consumer Information</u>

http://www.consumer.gov
http://www.pueblo.gsa.gov
http://www.fcc.gov/Consumers
http://www.cpsc.gov
http://www.ftc.gov

Uncle Sam's contribution to consumer affairs includes sites devoted to the latest scam and fraud news, the Consumer Information Center, telecommunications service fraud, Consumer Product Safety Council and the Federal Trade Commission.

122
<u>Better Business Bureau</u>

http://www.bbb.org

File a complaint online, find your local Bureau, get information on a company and read the latest news and alerts related to fraud.

123
E-Complaints

http://www.ecomplaints.com

If you've ever tried to complain and no one listened, this is the site for you. Not only will your complaint be heard, it will be posted for others to see and will be forwarded through the appropriate chain of authority to help you get results.

124
Internet Hoaxes

http://kumite.com/myths
http://www.hoaxkill.com
http://www.911virusalert.com

Next time you get an e-mail warning of some devastating computer virus, look it up at one of these sites. It's probably just a hoax, but why take a chance?

125
Remove Me From Your List

http://optout.cdt.org

Junk mail can be a waste of time and resources. This site has a step-by-step guide to removing yourself from these mailing lists.

CHAPTER VI
SOLD ON THE NET

126
Mall Fever

http://www.reallybigmall.com
http://www.mall41.com
A typical shopping mall has about 200 stores. This mall has over 1,800 stores and even allows you to create your own online mall for free.

127
Shopping Spot

http://www.shoppingspot.com
Here's your spot for learning and identifying great places to shop on the Net.

128
Best Deals Online

http://www.mysimon.com
http://www.dealtime.com
http://www.pricewatch.com
http://www.pricescan.com
http://www.bottomdollar.com

Wouldn't it be great to have your very own personal shopper who knows exactly where to get the best deals? Here are some good ones, and you don't have to pay anything for the service.

129
Buy the Book

http://www.alibris.com
http://www.amazon.com
http://www.bn.com
http://www.gutenberg.net

Whether you're looking for a current best seller, a classic that is difficult to find or a book that is in the public domain, these sites have millions of books for you.

130
Flowers

http://www.flowerbud.com
http://www.proflowers.com
It's easy to order magnificent flowers on the Net and receive them by FedEx.

131
GoTo Shopping

http://shop.goto.com
This is an easy-to-use shopping comparison site. Click on what you want to buy, then specify a price range and other factors to narrow your choices down to a few.

132
Shop 'Til You Drop

http://www.shop.com
http://www.shopping.com
http://www.shoponline123.com
Next time you want to go shopping online, remember these addresses.

133
<u>Gift Certificates</u>

http://www.giftpoint.com
http://www.giftcertificates.com
These sites sell gift certificates for many stores.

134
<u>Elder Gift Ideas</u>

http://www.eldergift.com
http://www.seniorstore.com
Here are some places to turn if you're looking for great gift ideas for seniors. Tell your friends, and maybe you'll get a present from them.

135
<u>Paper or Plastic?</u>

http://www.peapod.com
http://www.homegrocer.com
http://www.webvan.com
Get groceries delivered to your house with the click of a mouse.

136
Crafts on the Net

http://www.crafts.com
If you knit, stitch, mold, paint or weave, these sites will have something for you.

137
Coupons Make Cents

http://www.valpak.com
http://www.hotcoupons.com
http://www.coupons.com
http://www.coolsavings.com
These are fantastic resources for coupon clippers. Just print and save.

138
Cars on the Web

http://www.cars.com
http://www.autobytel.com
http://www.carsdirect.com
Buy a car on the Web without the haggling, fuss or pressure.

139
Name Brand Auctions

http://www.ebay.com
http://auctions.amazon.com
http://auctions.yahoo.com
These are all excellent person-to-person auctions where you can buy and sell almost anything you want.

140
Addicted to Auctions

http://www.auctioninsider.com
http://www.auctionuniverse.com
http://www.auctionbeagle.com
http://www.searchandfound.com
http://www.biddersedge.com
Here are some more sites to feed the auction bug. Browse awhile; who knows what you'll find?

141
Auction Fever

http://www.boxlot.com
http://www.itrack.com
http://www.auctionrover.com
http://www.auctionwatch.com
http://www.auctionpatrol.com

Whether it's on Ebay or any of the other auction sites, these sites will assist with tracking and watching the auction action.

142
Everything is Negotiable

http://www.haggle.com
http://www.hagglezone.com
http://www.makeusanoffer.com

Do you enjoy bargaining? Go ahead, enter the haggle zone online.

143
Get it for Free

http://www.free.com
http://www.freeshop.com

There are many free things on the Net; these sites lead you in the right direction.

144
Free Phone Calls

http://weblink.i-link.net
http://www.phonefree.com
http://www.dialpad.com
http://www.net2phone.com
These sites provide the ability to make free phone calls via the Internet.

145
Fax for Free

http://www.mail.com
http://www.efax.com
Visit these sites to get free e-mail, a free fax number for sending and receiving faxes by e-mail and the ability to receive voice mail through your e-mail.

CHAPTER VII
GET OUT OF TOWN

146
Portals to Travel

http://www.kasbah.com
http://www.johnnyjet.com
http://www.tripspot.com
These travel search engines and directories contain all the information you need to plan your next trip.

147
Travel with the Best

http://www.concierge.com
http://www.thetrip.com
http://www.travelocity.com
http://expedia.msn.com
Use these premier travel sites to research trips and to make travel arrangements.

148
Name Your Price

http://www.priceline.com
Priceline is the pioneer in customer-initiated pricing. You specify what you are willing to pay, and you could—if your offer is accepted—get a great deal.

149
Travel Bargains

http://www.bestfares.com
http://www.cheaptickets.com
http://www.economytravel.com
http://www.lowestfare.com
http://www.lowairfare.com
http://www.air-fare.com
Do a little research at these sites, and try to get the best fare.

150
Fodors

http://www.fodors.com
Visit this site to create your own customized travel guide. Hundreds of destinations around the globe are covered.

151
Budget Travel Online

http://www.frommers.com
Travel expert Arthur Frommer provides details, travel tips, numerous travel-related resources, discount travel information, cruise details and such interesting sections as "Cheapest Places on Earth" and "Senior Specials."

152
Lonely Planet

http://www.lonelyplanet.com
For insightful travel reviews about destinations all across the globe, this is a good source to consult.

153
Medicine Planet

http://www.travelhealth.com
http://www.medicineplanet.com
http://www.drwisetravel.com
These sites provide priceless health information for today's worldwide travelers. A special section for seniors includes health risk assessment for specific countries and expert information for travelers with special needs.

154
CitySearch

http://www.citysearch.com
http://www.digitalcity.com
http://www.usacitylink.com
These sites offer detailed information about cities throughout the world. Just select a city and start surfing. When you're finished, you'll feel as if you've already been there.

155
State Connection

http://www.50states.com
http://www.officialcitysites.org
Before your next trip, visit these sites to learn more about the cities and states. You'll find interesting official information and also some offbeat stuff.

156
Maps Galore

http://www.mapblast.com
http://www.mapquest.com
http://www.mapsonus.com
From maps to driving directions, these sites will keep you on the right road.

157
Smarter Living
http://www.smarterliving.com/senior
Live smarter with these travel tips and deals specifically for seniors. Sign up to have travel bargains sent to you by e-mail.

158
Great Places to Stay
http://www.placestostay.com
If you're looking for lodging, this site is ready with thousands of suggestions.

159
Home Exchange
http://www.homexchange.com
http://www.seniorshomeexchange.com
These sites allow members to exchange homes with each other. It's a great way to meet new friends and save money.

160
Home Free

http://www.homefree.com

This site helps save money and increase travel enjoyment worldwide by matching people who want to trade homes, finding free or low-cost accommodations and assisting those who seek travel companions.

161
Elderhostel

http://www.elderhostel.org

Elderhostel has more than 25 years of experience specializing in quality, affordable, educational travel for adults 55 and older. Share ideas and explore new places.

162
Virtually There

http://www.virtuallythere.com

Just input your Sabre reservation code and a last name, and VirtuallyThere will show you a complete, ready-to-print itinerary.

163
Inside the Park

http://www.recreation.gov
http://www.llbean.com/parksearch
http://parks.yahoo.com
http://www.nps.gov
http://www.blm.gov/education
If you want to explore some magnificent parks, here are thousands listed for you.

164
Passenger Rights

http://www.passengerrights.com
Got a travel complaint? Want to read about other peoples' issues? This site deals with everything related to passenger rights.

165
Pets Welcome

http://www.petswelcome.com
Pets Welcome contains a list of pet-friendly hotels, motels, bed & breakfasts and campsites. You'll also find pet travel tips and a listing of vets and kennels.

"Now that I'm retired, you know what I miss most?
I miss daydreaming about my retirement."

166
Travel Secrets
http://www.travelsecrets.com
Visit this site for helpful travel tips, bargain alerts and more. Make sure you go to the Top Secrets department.

167
Travel Zoo Top 20
http://www.travelzoo.com
Every week, Travel Zoo scours more than 200 companies for the "Top 20 Travel Deals on the Net." Read it here or sign up to have the Top 20 e-mailed to you weekly.

168
Military Hops
http://www.ee.umd.edu/medlab/spacea/spacea.html
If you're an active, reserve or retired member of the military, this site will explain how you can take advantage of the military's "space available" bargain flying program.

169
Hit the Road

http://www.aaa.com
http://www.motorists.org
http://www.speedtrap.org
http://www.speedtrap.com
These sites will help you when you plan to travel by car.

170
Roadside America

http://www.roadsideamerica.com
http://www.roadsidepeek.com
Though the interstate highway system has diminished roadside travel, there is still a lot of America to experience on these back roads.

171
From Chicago to L.A.

http://www.route66magazine.com
http://www.route66.com
These sites will help you get your kicks on Route 66.

172
Amtrak

http://www.amtrak.com
If you want to ride the rails, this site will keep you on track. Find routes, review schedules, buy tickets and more. Click on the "special offers" link to learn about senior discounts.

173
Embark Here

http://www.cruising.org
http://www.fieldingtravel.com/cf/index.htm
http://www.travelon.com/cruises
These sites specialize in cruise ship travel. If you're ready, this is the way to sail.

174
Embassy Web

http://www.embassyweb.com
Here's a good place to find phone numbers, Web sites and e-mail addresses of foreign embassies around the world.

175
Language of the Land

http://www.travlang.com
http://world.altavista.com
http://www.freetranslation.com
Heading for a foreign destination? These sites are well known for their language translation tools.

176
Currency Converter

http://www.oanda.com
http://www.x-rates.com
Make sure you know the money exchange rates of any countries you plan to visit.

177
World Time

http://www.worldtimeserver.com
Use this site to find out what time it is anywhere in the world.

178
Travel Warnings

http://travel.state.gov/travel_warnings.html
This U.S. State Department site will tell you about some places to avoid due to health concerns, political unrest or just plain lousy weather.

179
Be a Courier

http://www.aircourier.org
http://www.wallstech.com
Couriers escort packages to destinations and usually receive significant discounts on their travel expenses. Visit these sites to learn about becoming a courier.

180
Virtual Move

http://www.move.com
http://www.virtualrelocation.com
If you're on the move, use these sites before you pack. They offer virtual city tours, real estate information, city comparisons, community profiles and other tools to become an informed mover.

CHAPTER VIII
POLITICALLY AWARE

181
Volunteer Match

http://www.volunteermatch.org
Want to become an involved citizen? This site utilizes the power of the Internet to help individuals — nationwide — find volunteer opportunities posted through local nonprofit and public sector organizations.

182
Online Voter Registration

http://www.beavoter.com
Organized by AARP, America Online and MCI WorldCom, this non-partisan, non-profit effort's mission is to "harness the simplicity and innovative nature of the Internet to increase voter participation in the United States."

183
The Seniors Coalition

http://www.senior.org

The Seniors Coalition is a non-profit advocacy group that represents important issues concerning America's senior citizens. Visit this site to identify and learn more about the issues that are important to you.

184
Committee on Aging

http://www.senate.gov/~aging

Visit the United States Senate Committee on Aging to read about major concerns.

185
Be Heard

http://www.vote.com
http://www.becounted.com

These sites ask your opinions on a wide range of topics and forward those opinions to the appropriate lawmakers.

186
Seniors Say!

http://www.seniorsurvey.com
Designed specifically for seniors, this site provides a forum where they can easily speak their minds and be heard.

187
Political Information

http://www.politicalinformation.com
Here you'll find a wealth of political information, tools and links to thousands of Web sites related to politics, policy and political news.

188
All About Politics

http://www.politics.com
http://www.allpolitics.com
Get current political news from these sites.

189
Follow the Money
http://www.opensecrets.org
This is your online source for money in politics. Find out who's on the giving and receiving ends.

190
Speak Up
http://www.govote.com
http://www.speakout.com
Developed at a grassroots level, these sites address the issues of the day and contain detailed political information.

191
C-SPAN
http://www.cspan.org
You've watched them on cable, and now you have access to public affairs on the Web.

192
Polling Report
http://www.pollingreport.com
This site tracks trends in public opinion. What are your opinions?

193
White House

http://www.whitehouse.gov

Take a virtual tour of the most famous residence in the country. Go right into he Oval Office; the President won't mind. You can even rummage around in the White House Library and sneak into the White House pressroom.

194
Congress

http://www.senate.gov
http://www.house.gov
http://www.congress.org
http://www.capweb.net

These extremely useful sites are packed with information that can help you identify and contact the politicians that represent you. Helpful search tools, contact information, Capitol Hill news, legislative issues and more can be found here.

195
The Last Word

http://www.supremecourtus.gov
http://www.findlaw.com/casecode/supreme.html

Visit the Supreme Court, and read all of its opinions.

196
Legislative Issues

http://thomas.loc.gov
http://www.aarp.org/legislativeguide
Stay current on important political issues. Find out about upcoming votes, pending legislation and all about your U.S. Representative's voting record.

197
Let's Party

http://www.democrats.org
http://www.rnc.org
http://www.reformparty.org
http://www.lp.org
Consider these sites to be Party Central; Democrats, Republicans, Reform and Libertarians are all in attendance.

198
Political Cartoons

http://www.politicalcartoons.com
Politics can be funny, and these professional cartoonists are tuned in to the issues.

CHAPTER IX
KNOWLEDGE IS POWER

199
Knowledge Zoo

http://www.zooba.com
Zooba says, "Our free service is based on the simple idea that no matter who you are, you can always be smarter. And Zooba makes getting smarter easy."

200
Headline News

http://www.1stheadlines.com
http://www.frontpagedailynews.com
http://www.headlinenews.com
Get a quick dose of news at these sites.

201
Customized News

http://www.individual.com
http://www.newshub.com
http://www.crayon.net
One of the great services provided by many Web sites is the ability to customize the news and information that you receive.

202
Network News

http://abcnews.go.com
http://cbsnews.cbs.com
http://www.msnbc.com
http://www.cnn.com
http://www.foxnews.com
http://www.bbc.co.uk
The major networks have complete and timely news on the Net.

203
Weekly News

http://www.newsweek.com
http://www.time.com
http://www.usnews.com
It's time for your weekly news from Newsweek, Time and U.S. News and World Report.

204
Inform and Serve

http://www.apbnews.com
This is a source for news, information and data on crime, justice and safety.

205
Reader's Digest

http://www.readersdigest.com
This classic publication has made a very smooth landing online.

206
The Paperboy Delivers

http://www.thepaperboy.com
http://www.totalnews.com
With more than 4,000 newspapers available, you might need another pot of coffee.

207
Seniors' Writing Workshop
http://www.mbnet.mb.ca/crm/crm/lynch1.html
Write on! Take all that incredible information, knowledge and experience that you have and put it down in words.

208
Newsletters
http://www.topica.com
http://www.backwire.com
http://www.infobeat.com
Receiving newsletters and current information via e-mail is a great way to view Web sites. Use these to keep up to date.

209
Tipped Off
http://www.tipworld.com
http://www.dummiesdaily.com
Get daily newsletters from professional resources on hundreds of subjects.

210
Discuss It

http://www.liszt.com
http://www.deja.com/usenet
People on the Net enjoy sharing their opinions, thoughts and expertise.

211
The Search is On

http://www.altavista.com
http://www.yahoo.com
http://www.google.com
http://www.excite.com
http://www.lycos.com
Though the results from search engines can sometimes be overwhelming, you may
want to use one or more of these popular ones.

212
Multiple Search Engines

http://www.locate.com
http://www.northernlight.com
http://www.metacrawler.com
http://www.profusion.com

They go by the fancy name of meta-search engines. Simply put, these sites will quickly search many search engines at one time.

213
Social Security Death Index

http://ssdi.genealogy.rootsWeb.com

The power of the Internet allows you to search though more than 60 million records to find Social Security numbers, dates of birth and death, last known residences and more. This is a great tool for genealogy projects.

214
E-mail a Friend

http://people.yahoo.com
http://www.whowhere.lycos.com
http://www.bigfoot.com
http://www.switchboard.com
http://www.theultimates.com
Look for anyone's e-mail address or phone number by using these search engines.

215
Reverse Look-ups

http://www.anywho.com
http://www.infospace.com/info/reverse.htm
Type in a phone number, and get a name and address. Type in a name, and get an address and phone number. Type in an address, and get names and phone numbers. You get the idea.

216
Do You Have the Time?

http://www.time.gov
http://www.timeanddate.com
We can't guarantee you'll arrive on time, but we can assure you that you'll know exactly what time it is.

217
Area Code Decoder

http://decoder.americom.com
Type in an area code, and the city will be displayed.

218
Package Tracker

http://www.packtrack.com
Whether you send it FedEx, UPS, DHL, Emery, Express Mail, Airborne or Purorlator, you can track it here.

219
Look It Up!

http://www.britannica.com
Encyclopedia Britannica has done an excellent job categorizing the Internet. Quench your thirst for knowledge here.

220
Reference Desk

http://www.refdesk.com
Bob Drudge's site refers to itself as "The best single source for facts on the Net."

221
It's My Opinion

http://writ.findlaw.com
Direct from one of the major legal sites on the Net, here are opinions on laws and issues that affect us all.

222
Discovery Online

http://www.discovery.com
The joy of exploration and discovery can be found at this site designated as "tools for everyday adventures."

223
Marvelous Exploration

http://www.explorezone.com
Earth, space, weather and other science marvels are explained here. They didn't teach science this way when we were kids.

224
Out of This World

http://hubble.stsci.edu
http://www.skypub.com
http://www.space.com
http://www.nasm.edu
Peer into the cosmos with the help of these heavenly sites.

225
Earth From Space

http://earth.jsc.nasa.gov
Considered to be a national treasure by many, this site contains a quarter-million photographs taken by the men and women who have been fortunate enough to travel away from our planet.

226
Exploritorium
http://www.exploratorium.edu
Visit the museum of science, art and human perception.

227
How Does it Work?
http://www.howstuffworks.com
Glad you asked. This site takes great pride in explaining mysteries of everyday life.

228
Share the Knowledge
http://www.circleoflearning.com
Circle of Learning is devoted to enriching the lives of people over 50. Read, learn, teach and tell stories.

229
Learn 2
http://www.learn2.com
Learn to do almost anything at this site. Over a thousand subject areas are covered.

230
Where Were You?

http://www.wherewereyou.com

Do you remember where you were when Neil Armstrong made that "one small step for man?" This site publishes personal accounts of where people were and what they were doing on July 20, 1969.

231
The Apollo Lunar Surface Journal

http://www.hq.nasa.gov/alsj

This is a superbly crafted Web site documenting each of the missions to the Moon. Audio and video clips, photos, transcripts, debriefing notes, commentary from many of the astronauts and more are included.

232
Soundtrack for a Century

http://www.millennium.sonymusic.com

Sony Music has created a masterful 20th Century retrospective, featuring the music of nearly 500 artists along with videos, photos and more. It's a mesmerizing glimpse at the past using the technology of today.

233
Great Achievements
http://www.greatachievements.org
The National Academy of Engineering presents an interesting look at the 20th Century's greatest engineering achievements. Explore this site, and learn how engineering shaped a century and changed the world.

234
Lost & Found Sound
http://www.lostandfoundsound.com
The folks at NPR have gathered a captivating collection of sound bites from the 20th Century.

235
Time Capsule
http://www.dmarie.com/timecap
What happened in history on the day you were born? Here's a quick, easy and fun way to find out.

236
The Greatest Generation
http://4worldwarii.4anything.com
People from the World War II era have been called the greatest generation. Here's to all the brave men and women who served.

237
WWII Aircraft and Pilots
http://www.militaryaviation.com
http://www.cebudanderson.com
http://home.att.net/~C.C.Jordan/index.html
http://www.westnet.com/~ssherman/index.html
Here's superb online documentation of the aircraft and young flyers that served their country so well. These are their words, photos and stories.

238
Dad's War
http://members.aol.com/dadswar
This Web site offers a complete, step-by-step guide to finding and telling your father's war stories through actual war records.

239
D-Day

http://www.dday.org
This site is home to the National D-Day Memorial Foundation, which is working to build and maintain a memorial to Allied Forces who invaded the Normandy coast of France on June 6, 1944.

240
Enola Gay

http://www.theenolagay.com
On the morning of August 6, 1945, Colonel Paul W. Tibbets flew the Enola Gay into history. This is his story.

241
Mighty Mo

http://www.ussmissouri.com
The USS Missouri is now permanently moored near the Arizona Memorial in Pearl Harbor, Hawaii. Visit this site to learn about this historic ship and all it represents.

242
Vietnam Memorial

http://www.no-quarter.org
http://www.thevirtualwall.org
Use the searchable database to find the name of a friend or loved one on "The Wall."
Nearly sixty thousand names are inscribed, each one representing a son or daughter,
mother or father, brother or sister or friend whose life was lost, but not forgotten.

243
Vietnam War Stories

http://www.war-stories.com
This award-winning Web site is a place where veterans of Vietnam can come and
share their memories. Nearly 300 war stories are currently posted.

244
Vietnam Tribute

http://www.vietvet.org
Within these pages can be found heartfelt tributes, remembrances, memorials,
stories and more, all dedicated to those who fought and died in Vietnam.

245
Korean War

http://korea50.army.mil
This site commemorates the Korean War veterans and provides visitors with an understanding and appreciation of the history of that conflict.

246
Desert Storm.

http://www.desert-storm.com
A student created this site, which is dedicated to Desert Storm vets. You'll also find details of the war, photos and links to other sites.

247
Military Buddy Locators

http://www.goatlocker.org
http://www.silverlance.com/audiover/buddies.htm
If you're trying to get in touch with a military buddy, here are a couple of great places to start your search.

248
Military Connection

http://www.va.gov
http://www.militaryconnections.com
http://www.military.com
http://www.militaryhub.com
http://www.veterans.com
http://www.uso.org
Here's to all the people who have served in the military.

249
Military Search Engine

http://www.searchmil.com
This search engine is dedicated to the military.

250
History Place

http://www.historyplace.com
From the American Revolution to the Impeachment of Bill Clinton, this site has it all. Dozens of thought-provoking presentations make this site a keeper.

251
U.S. History

http://www.ushistory.org
Brush up on your American history with guided tours, photos, informative articles and more. The lessons are entertaining, educational and brief and really come in handy if you weren't paying attention in history class.

CHAPTER X
FUN AND LEISURE

252
Nick at Night and TV Land

http://www.nick-at-nite.com
http://desiluweb.com/TVLand
Nick at Night and TV Land feature sound clips, trivia, actor bios, games and more for all the great TV shows. You'll find Adam 12, Alfred Hitchcock Presents, All in the Family, Dobie Gillis, Dragnet, The Honeymooners, I Love Lucy and much more.

253
Old Time Radio

http://www.dccomics.com/radio
Gather 'round the radio. It's time to listen to the "Man of Steel." Even if you don't want to hear the show, you'll enjoy seeing the old-time family photo.

254
Groucho on the Web
http://www.groucho-marx.com
http://www.groucho.com
http://www.marx-brothers.org
Here's an example of the wit and wisdom of Groucho Marx: "Age is not a particularly interesting subject. Anyone can get old. All you have to do is live long enough."

255
Who's on First?
http://www.city-net.com/abbottandcostellofc
This is the official Abbott & Costello home page. You'll find fan club information, biographies, sound clips (including Who's on First?) film info, products and more.

256
Moe, Larry, and Curly
http://www.threestooges.com
This is "the official site for knuckleheads." Spread out!

"When I said let's put some sizzle back into our marriage, he cooked me some bacon."

257
No Respect

http://www.rodney.com
Rodney Dangerfield was one of the first celebrities on the World Wide Web with jokes, sound bites, movie clips and more.

258
Norma Jean

http://www.marilynmonroe.com
She's gone, but never forgotten. Visit the official Web site of Marilyn Monroe.

259
Hooray for Hollywood

http://www.imdb.com
http://mrshowbiz.go.com
If you can't find it here, it has probably never been shown on the silver screen. These comprehensive movie databases contain everything there is to know about movies.

260
Oops

http://www.movie-mistakes.com
http://www.moviebloopers.com
These sites have thousands of documented movie mistakes, which prove that even movie stars are human.

261
Movie Trailers and More

http://www.movie-trailers.com
http://www.videoseeker.com
You'll find movie trailers, television clips, news and more. Don't forget your popcorn.

262
It's Movie Time

http://www.movielink.com
http://www.moviefone.com
http://www.allmovie.com
Where's it playing and at what time? These sites will help you make the right choice when going to the movies.

263
Movie Reviews and News

http://www.juxtaposeur.com
http://www.flickfilosopher.com
http://www.aint-it-cool-news.com

If you want to know what someone else thought about a film, here are some unique and original points of view.

264
Get the Clicker

http://www.tvguide.com
http://www.zap2it.com

Type in your zip code, and you'll be zapped into TV land.

265
Comics on the Web

http://www.comics.com
http://www.dccomics.com
http://www.lil-abner.com

More than 100 comics—from Alley Oop to Ziggy—can be found here. There's Peanuts, Superman, Dilbert and more.

266
Editorial Cartoons
http://www.cagle.com
Do you enjoy the editorial cartoons in your local paper? This site has thousands of cartoons from the best cartoonists in the world.

267
Classic Commercials
http://adage.com/news_and_features/special_reports/commercials
Here are Advertising Age's fifty best commercials, dating back to the 1940s.

268
Pet Projects
http://www.411pets.com
http://www.akc.org
http://www.thepetvine.com
http://www.doghause.com
These sites will allow you to enjoy your pets even more.

269
Gardener's Delight

http://www.gardenweb.com
http://www.garden.com
http://www.bhglive.com/gardening/db/findhome.htm
http://www.yardcare.com
http://www.vg.com
http://www.gardenguides.com
http://www.gardenreview.com

Visit these sites to make your gardening knowledge grow. Get gardening tips, sign up for newsletters, browse through the gardening encyclopedia and even enter your zip code to find out what you should be growing now.

270
Send a Greeting

http://www.bluemountain.com
http://www.americangreetings.com
http://www.regards.com
http://www.123greetings.com
http://www.digitalcard.com

These very popular sites let you send free, entertaining, e-greetings to your friends and family. Pick from a wide range of occasions and holidays.

271
Fun Cards

http://www.gigglegarden.com
http://www.funsilly.com

Send animated greeting cards to your friends.

272
Dinner is Served

http://www.gourmetspot.com
http://www.tubears.com/gourmet
http://www.recipe.com
http://www.goodcooking.com
http://www.starchef.com
http://www.kitchenlink.com

Nobody has figured out how to send food through a modem, but these sites are the next best things, with expert cooking tips, world-class recipes, cookbooks and more.

273
My Recipes

http://www.mymenus.com

Need a recipe? This site has them by category, ingredient, nutritional content and a list of the most popular ones.

274
Zagat Guides
http://www.zagat.com
If cooking is not on your personal agenda tonight, Zagat's—the world leader in rating restaurants—will be happy to give you some good recommendations.

275
Museums
http://www.museumnetwork.com
Over 33,000 museums are listed in this network. Go for a visit and enjoy all the culture the world has to offer.

276
National Portrait Gallery
http://www.npg.si.edu
The bricks-and-mortar National Portrait Gallery will be closed for renovations until 2003. However, its outstanding collection is available to you here online.

277
Listen Up!

http://www.timecast.com
http://www.broadcast.com
The Net has become a great broadcast medium. These sites serve as portals to some of the amazing topics you can listen to.

278
Let's Listen

http://www.com
With more than a quarter-million songs in their library, these folks are bound to have just the music you're looking for.

279
All Things Considered…

http://www.npr.org
…this is one of the best places to go for news, information and music on the Net.

280
All Music

http://www.allmusic.com

This is the world's largest music database. Just type in an artist's name and see everything he or she ever recorded, the names of all the players in the band and everything they recorded and more. Type in a song title, and see everyone who recorded it. If you're a music fan, this is an enlightening experience.

281
What's Your Sign?

http://www.horoscopes.com
http://www.astrology.com
http://www.freehoroscopes.net
http://www.excite.com/horoscopes

"You are an explorer. You take chances. You're not afraid to use new technologies. You like to surf the Net and find out what the stars have in store for you." Have some fun and see what's in store for you.

282
Genealogy

http://www.cyndislist.com
http://www.rootsweb.com
http://www.familysearch.org
http://www.familytree.com
http://www.familytreemaker.com
http://www.genhomepage.com
http://www.genealogy.com
http://www.genealogytoolbox.com

Genealogy is one of the major hobbies on the Net. These sites let you search for your ancestral records and create family trees.

283
Crossword Puzzles

http://www.bestcrosswords.com
http://www.dailycrossword.com
http://www.oneacross.com
http://www.wordcross.net

What's a three-letter word that describes a good time? Visit these sites to find out.

284
It's a Classic

http://hoyle.won.net
Hearts, Spades, Bridge and more are available at this site.

285
Puzzle Depot

http://www.puzzledepot.com
More than just puzzles, this site is loaded with trivia games, word games, brain blitz, bingo and more.

286
Gettin' Jiggy

http://www.jigzone.com
If you like jigsaw puzzles, visit this site to see how much fun they are online.

287
Checkmate

http://www.itsyourturn.com
http://www.chessclub.com
http://www.chesslab.com
Play by yourself or join others online. These sites have something for all chess fans.

288
BINGO

http://www.bingo.com
http://www.bingoonline.com
Say it loud and clear: BINGO!

289
Vegas

http://www.virtualvegas.com
It's the next best thing to being there.

"They've made online shopping so much like
the real thing, after visiting 20 stores I'm
exhausted and my feet hurt!"

290
Java Games

http://www.darkfish.com
This is a very fun collection of popular games online, including checkers. They're easy to play, but hard to win.

291
You Win!

http://www.iwin.com
http://www.extremelotto.com
http://www.huronline.com
http://www.gamesville.com
Play your favorite games. If you're lucky, you can win prizes. Best of all, it's free.

292
Quizland

http://www.quizland.com
If you've got the time, they've got the games — quizzes, trivia, puzzles and more.

293
Totally Trivia

http://www.absolutetrivia.com

If you're into trivia, this site will provide more than 10,000 searchable factoids.

294
Millionaire

http://heavy.etv.go.com

Join Regis online during one of America's favorite game shows. Play along with the contestants on TV, and answer the same questions they're answering. You can't win a million, but you will have lots of fun.

295
Solitaire Anyone?

http://www.solitairegames.com

If solitaire is your game, you'll have fun here with over a hundred kinds.

296
Bridge Information

http://www.cbf.ca/GBL/GBLplay.html
http://www.bridgetoday.com
If you're interested in bridge, visit these sites for tips, links, news and more.

297
Hit Me!

http://www.blackjackinfo.com
http:/www.allaboutblackjack.com
Learn to play Blackjack like a pro—strategies, tips and rules.

298
Cameras Around the World

http://www.earthcam.com
http://www.cammunity.com
http://www.camcity.com
It's almost as good as being there. From truly interesting locations to the bizarre, you'll find cameras spanning the globe.

299
Family Reunions

http://www.myfamily.com
http://www.ecircles.com
http://www.myevents.com
http://www.familypoint.com

These sites let you establish your own place on the Web where friends and family can visit and chat and post stories, news items, photos and more.

300
Class Reunion

http://www.classmates.com

Looking for your former classmates? You may find them here. Enter your name, year of graduation and high school.

Index (by site number)

INDEX (BY SITE NUMBER)

INDEX (BY SITE NUMBER)

The Incredible Newsletter

If you are enjoying this book, you can also arrange to receive a steady stream of more "incredible Internet things," delivered directly to your e-mail address.

The Leebow Letter, Ken Leebow's weekly e-mail newsletter, provides new sites, updates on existing ones and information about other happenings on the Internet.

For more details about *The Leebow Letter* and how to subscribe, visit us at:

WWW.300INCREDIBLE.COM

(USO) United Service Organizations

For nearly 60 years, the United Service Organizations (USO) has "Delivered America" to service members stationed around the world, thousands of miles from family and friends. The USO provides celebrity entertainment, recreation, cultural orientation, language training, travel assistance, telephone and Internet access, and other vital services to military personnel and their families at 115 locations worldwide. The USO is a non-profit organization, not a government agency. It relies on the generosity of corporations and individuals to enable its programs and services to continue. For more information on contributing to the USO, please call 1-800-876-7469 or visit its Web site at www.uso.org.